# WE ARE FRIENDS

BY KRISTI T. BUTLER
ILLUSTRATED BY MICHAEL GREJNIEC

**Harcourt**

Orlando   Boston   Dallas   Chicago   San Diego

Visit *The Learning Site!*
**www.harcourtschool.com**

We like running.

We like jumping.

We like drawing.

We like reading.

We like swimming.

We like riding.

Requests for permission to make copies of any part of the work should be mailed to the following address: School Permissions, Harcourt, Inc., 6277 Sea Harbor Drive, Orlando, Florida 32887-6777.

HARCOURT and the Harcourt Logo are trademarks of Harcourt, Inc.

Printed in the United States of America

ISBN 0-15-314280-4

6 7 8 9 10 069 08 07 06 05 04